IT MAY HAPPEN TO YOU

TRUE STORY

CHANDERKIRAN RADHAKRISHAN NANDA

ISBN

Hardcase 979-8-89588-909-1
Paperback 979-8-89556-809-5

Contents

Introduction

This is the true story of my visit to the country known as "Land of Rising Sun". I am sure you must have guessed which country it is. I am writing this small book for everyone who visits this country for any reason. Things that happen to me may happen to anyone.

When I left my home, I had prepared a huge list of activities I would do. As a technocrat, I wanted to know what latest technology is being developed. I had prepared a good list of shopping. Having read for its technical advancement I was excited to meet some interesting people. But sadly, everything remained a dream.

What I thought or what I gathered was wrong. It was disgusting but I always followed three principles of Gautam Budha: ***Truth, Benevolence and Tolerance***. I also believe people in this country are religious and worship Budha. But even that perception was wrong. As for myself I do not pray or go to any specific temple, but I respect every religion. I noticed a typical person here does not spend too much time in Temples etc. Rather I must say life here is like an automated routine. Everyone is running for survival. One can notice the stress on the majority of people.

If you have not guessed the country's name, let me give you some more hints. This country is located in the East of Asia. It is also famous by the name of Nippon by its country people. The country is famous all over the world because of its advanced technology.

Why is it known as the "Land of Rising Sun"? This name is called because the sun rises first here and then in any other part of the world. Talking about it is like talking about a country which is perfect on its own. It has one of the most advanced technologies. The country has the highest literacy rate in the whole world. It is formed from about 6,852 islands and falls in the continent of Asia. This country records the lowest crime rate every year compared to other countries. The people are best known for maintaining a better and healthier lifestyle that's why they are expected to live longer and happier lifestyle. There are more than 100 active volcanoes one can find here. Mount Fuji, which is also these people's sacred or religious spot, is the tallest Mountain found here. The country has few resources available, but Coal, Iron, Zinc, and Lead are still abundant. No doubt, that the country is fully equipped with modern amenities which is why it has the most vending machines present in the whole world. The country has a constitutional monarchical government with Parliamentary Government. The country has its economy third in the whole world.

If you have not guessed it is Japan. In the the next few chapters, I have written real facts I had experienced. I had no intention of speaking low of any country, people, or culture. I am sure some of the feedback will be looked into seriously by concerned agencies and corrective action. As you read through this book you will find some sentences highlighted and in Italics. These are some important points, which the authorities must look into for the progress/development of the country. The views expressed are my own and some maybe wrong when looked at from others perspective. My planned trip was initially for 10 days. However due to circumstances beyond my control, it lasted for nine months and 17 days.

I am sure it will be an eye-opener for many who travel around the globe. This trip taught me many lessons of life. As you read through you will know the purpose of my visit, how one is trapped, and you will learn many things about Japan and Japanese people. You will also learn about the real facts of the Japanese judicial system. Japanese government officials do not disclose their names. They are referred by their badge numbers. I could not understand why names were not disclosed. Implementation of digital technology is poor. Orders are transmitted via hard copies. Signatures are not used, but finger impression along with individual authorized rubber stamp are used for approving decisions. This slows down the process to a large extent. But it must be appreciated the timelines are maintained strictly. In the present times when nothing is impossible one has a very big problem of language. 90 to 98% people do not speak

English nor do they understand English. Their knowledge of global world which I call geography is very poor. Most of them have never travelled out of Japan and are not aware there exists a life outside Japan. There is a high feeling of racism. They do not believe in their own systems and look upon everything with suspicion. I have given real examples as you read through. Inflation is high. Common items are expensive.

I hope you enjoy this reading. ***My sincere thanks to my legal team Tomohiro Shibao, San Yugo Fukumoto San and M/S. Eiffei.***

Your criticism/feedback will be very much appreciated, which may be sent to my email. ***chanradh7@gmail.com***

Chapter 1

Background and Purpose of Visit

Background:

In 2006, I had the opportunity to give a talk at a seminar in China focused on Digital Manufacturing. The event featured speakers from around the globe, and I represented India. It was a pleasure to meet individuals with diverse interests and expertise in various engineering fields. Unfortunately, I did not encounter any speakers from Japan. There were, however, participants from marketing and sales. The atmosphere was charged with excitement as everyone was busy with their final preparations. I observed many attendees engrossed in their laptops, refining their presentations. The seminar spanned two days, and my presentation was scheduled for the second day just before lunch. Having given similar talks regularly, I had little to prepare, which allowed me to observe others—some were nervous, some confused, and others diligently reviewing their presentation materials.

I noticed a gentleman sitting alone, struggling with his laptop. He was perspiring heavily, with sweat dripping from his forehead. Based on his skin colour, I guessed he might be from Africa. Observing him closely, I realized why he was isolated—his appearance, with a darker complexion, seemed to make others uncomfortable.

Feeling compelled to help, I approached him, drawing on my extensive experience with computers, laptops, and software. I introduced myself and mentioned that I noticed he was having trouble and seemed stressed. He introduced himself as Johnson from South Africa, a businessman dealing in spare parts and machinery for the automotive industry. He explained that his laptop wasn't booting, and he was unable to access his presentation, which was scheduled for the next day at 11 AM.

I offered to take a look at his HP laptop and, after running a diagnostic, discovered a hard disk failure. I asked if he had any money with him, and he confirmed that he did. I suggested we visit an HP dealer to purchase a new laptop and see if they could recover any data. I also offered to help him create a new presentation if he could provide his ideas. Relieved, he agreed, and we headed straight to the HP shop.

Around 3 PM, the HP technician informed us that his hard disk had failed, making recovery will be difficult and time-consuming. He decided to get a new laptop and I installed the operating system along with the complete suite of Microsoft Office. Fortunately, he had a hard copy of his previous PowerPoint presentation. We returned to the hotel and began recreating his presentation in PowerPoint. By the time we finished, it was nearly 3 AM. He did a trial run to ensure everything was working fine. I also mentioned that I would ask him a few questions after his presentation, which made him very happy and satisfied.

I felt very fulfilled helping someone I didn't know. After a hectic day, we sat down to talk about ourselves. We ordered some drinks and snacks, enjoying some single malt scotch. During our conversation, he opened up about his life. When I asked about his family, he said, "Mr. Nanda, if you were a woman, would you ever marry me considering my appearance?" It was clear he was aware of his shortcomings. He continued, "Mr. Nanda, I am 54 years old and all alone. I have no friends except for a few business contacts. You are the first person who has ever helped me, and I don't know why. I am so happy today that I can't express it. I always thought no one in this world cared about me, but your help has given me a new lease on life. If I ever die, I will leave my wealth to you." I didn't take it seriously, as people often say such things after a few drinks. I went to my room and slept happily, content that I had helped someone in need.

The next day was our big day. He delivered his presentation, and I asked him a few questions, which he answered confidently. Other participants also asked questions, and he responded well. My presentation followed his and was well-received, with many interesting questions.

An executive from Korea was very impressed and invited me to give a talk in Korea. The next day, he flew back to Johannesburg, while I was scheduled to fly to Singapore in the afternoon on my way back to India. This meeting with Mr. Johnson taught me a valuable lesson: money is not the ultimate source of happiness; human connections, friends, and companions are what truly matter.

We stayed in touch, and two years later, we met again at a conference in Kuala Lumpur. It was a pleasure to see Johnson, who held me in high regard. A few years after our meeting in KL, I received an email from a lawyer informing me that Johnson had passed away in a car accident and that I should contact Mr. Desmond Harvey. Given the prevalence of internet scams, I ignored the email.

However, on March 21, 2021, I received another email from Mr. Desmond Harvey. He mentioned Mr. Johnson and provided some background, stating that Johnson had left some funds for me, which had been moved to Japan. He advised me to contact his Account Officer, Rev. Dalibor Paul. When I reached out to Rev. Dalibor Paul, he requested 490 GBP to send me an ATM card. I refused to pay. Rev. Dalibor Paul then offered to cover my travel, stay, and meals in Japan if I could pick up the card in person.

I love traveling to new places, so I thought, even if I didn't get the ATM card, I could enjoy a trip to Japan for free. I accepted the offer, and the itinerary was arranged for me to travel to Japan. I applied for a tourist visa and received a ticket for the route Mumbai-Doha-Korea-Fukuoka. On the eve of my departure, Rev. Dalibor Paul informed me that one Mr. Michael, travelling from Ohio to Israel via Doha, would give me a small handbag containing some clothes as a gift for officials in Japan. I made it clear that I would inspect the bag thoroughly for any hidden items.

I made it clear that if I found anything suspicious, I would leave the bag in Doha. He agreed to this condition. I insisted on this because I had read many books describing various methods of smuggling drugs. All my communication with Rev. Dalibor was through email and WhatsApp, and I had all the messages saved on my mobile. While traveling from Pune to Mumbai, I received a message from Rev. Dalibor asking me to delete our messages. I deliberately chose not to delete any of them, thinking they might be useful if he tried to deceive me.

The excitement of visiting a new place overshadowed any suspicions of foul play. I looked at this travel opportunity with a sense of pure wonder and innocence, where everything feels fresh and full of possibilities. It felt like experiencing life with an open heart and a clear mind, free from cynicism or preconceived notions.

Chapter 2

Start of Unexpected Journey

I began my journey on February 6th, 2023, at 9 AM, traveling from Pune to Mumbai to catch my evening flight to Doha. The drive took about four and a half hours, giving me plenty of time to check in and complete all the necessary formalities at the airport. It was a pleasantly cool and sunny day, and the trip from Pune to Mumbai was smooth with moderate traffic. I arrived at Mumbai International Airport around 1:30 PM. As expected, the airport was bustling with travellers from all over the world. Being one of the busiest airports, security here is always stringent. To enter the departure hall, I had to join the queue and present my photo ID and valid ticket.

Once you enter the departure hall, one has to locate the check-in gate of airlines and stand in the queue. This process takes about an hour or so. Once checked in you, have to go through a security check which is again a wait in the long queue followed by immigration clearance. By the time all the formalities are completed, a couple of hours have passed and it is still a long walk to the departure gate.

My flight to Doha was scheduled for 6:30 PM, and I was already feeling tired.

I arrived in Doha on 6 February 2023, at 11:45 PM. Costa Coffee at Hamad International Airport in Doha was the place decided for my meeting with Mr. Micheal. At half past midnight, Mr. Michael, who was flying from Ohio to Israel via Doha, arrived and handed me the handbag. I immediately opened and emptied it. There were a few clothes, which I checked thoroughly for any hidden items in the pockets or seams. I also inspected the bag from all directions and did not notice anything unusual. I tapped the bag with my palm to see if it sounded different. Finally, I realized that since Mr. Michael had come from Ohio, the bag must have undergone customs scanning. So, I decided to carry the bag.

My connecting flight was operated by Qatar Airways which is known for its excellent hospitality. I enjoyed a few drinks and snacks before falling asleep, feeling exhausted.

My flight arrived in Seoul, Korea at 5:30 PM on 7 February 2023. At the arrival gate, I saw a staff member from Asiana Airlines holding a placard with my name. He escorted me to the next gate, as it was a long and complex walk. I would have missed my flight if it hadn't been for the Asiana staff. I boarded the aircraft and arrived at Fukuoka, Japan at 7.25 PM local time. I wasn't impressed with Asiana Airlines' hospitality and often compare it to Indian airlines. It was just average, nothing noteworthy.

I had completed the online check-out processes as instructed by the Japanese embassy in Mumbai to save time. When I arrived at the arrival hall, I noticed there was only one checked baggage in the whole flight and that was mine.

As I collected the baggage, one customs officer asked me to proceed to the customs counter for baggage inspection. Normal baggage inspection was done. Physically I was very tired as I was traveling for almost 36 hours. The customs officer emptied my checked-in baggage and also the hand baggage and took them for X-ray scanning. He came back and said we needed to go inside and do more detailed scanning.

I did not understand what was happening. Finally, he took me, along with the handbag I received from Mr. Michael, to the X-ray scanner. He showed me the scan and asked what it was. There was a black image appearing at the bottom of the bag. I admitted that I didn't know what it was. I then told the customs officer, "You are the expert who performs these scans every day, so you should be able to identify it." He said we have never seen such a scan. I then suggested, "Why don't you cut the bag open and find out what it is? I can give my consent in writing." The customs officer seemed hesitant, so I reiterated my willingness to cooperate fully. I provided my written consent, stating that I had no objections to them cutting open the bag to investigate the suspicious item.

There was one major problem, language. No one would speak any language other than the Japanese. I waited for 2 hours, tired, hungry and sleepy when they called an interpreter. She translated my consent from English to Japanese and they took the bag for cutting. As they cut open the bag, a few crystals, resembling sugar, spilled out. They conducted a chemical test, which revealed the presence of stimulants classified as banned drugs under Japanese drug control. They finally cut out the whole area and found a total quantity of crystals to be 1.915 KG.

The immediate comment from the customs officer as translated by the interpreter was **"We have never seen such precision engineering of hiding the material".** I said if experts like you cannot find out how do I know if something is hidden like this? This reflects the expertise of customs officers performing scanning day in and day out.

It was morning 4 AM Japanese local time. They confiscated all my belongings and detained me in police custody for further investigation. I was taken to the police detention centre. I was informed that they will interrogate me for 10 days. If required it may be extended by another 10 days. After a maximum period of 20 days, they will either acquit me or convict me. I requested them to let me call my family or at least let me send them a message. But the Japanese authorities outrightly refused my pleas.

I was left wondering what was meant by a **stimulant**. I asked the Japanese officer and no one knew what was the definition of a stimulant or rather they pretended not knowing. Language was going to be a challenge, so I found it wise to remain silent as much as possible.

Chapter 3

The Dawn of Difficult Times

Travelling had taken its toll on me. I was exhausted and wanted to get some rest. I begged officers to let me go to the hotel. I was supposed to handover the bag with the clothes to one Mr Steven. If they considered this serious, they needed to question Steven immediately to know more details about the stimulants. Mr. Steven was supposed to pay for my accommodation and meal expenses. But they did not take my advice for reasons best known to them. *I guessed that they were not serious about finding out where the stimulant was supposed to go*. But they were too excited to arrest me. I was taken to the police station and they completed the formalities of arrest. I was asked if I could hire a lawyer or needed one from their side. It was not practical for me to hire my own lawyer. But clarity dawned, revealing this as the beginning of an enduring cycle as even before I was produced in the court I was being asked to hire my lawyer.

Japan does follow Geneva convention but here they violate and term you as criminal even before any trial or investigation.

But every plea to reach out to my family back home was heartbreakingly denied. I requested them to inform the Indian Consulate in Japan which they said they will but was not done immediately. They took my belongings, including my medicines. I was then taken to the police detention centre and held there. I was given a room having no table or chair. I was given instructions to be followed with details of my daily routine. I was given bedding, toothbrush paste, soap, a towel and instructions on the daily routine. The food served was lacking in both quality and quantity.

My body couldn't tolerate the food, and I experienced a stomach upset right away. Unfortunately, there were no medical facilities at the detention centre, which was quite basic and lacked essential amenities. The staff seemed unprepared to handle medical emergencies, making it difficult to explain my situation and request medical attention. The language barrier and the overall environment added to the challenge, making it a very distressing experience.

After a day of persistent persuasion, I was finally taken to the hospital. Fortunately, at the hospital, I found a junior Indian doctor who could speak my native language. This was a huge relief amidst the chaos. He asked me about the medicines I had been carrying and informed me that one of them, 'Mobizox,' was banned in Japan. He explained that this medicine falls under the category of **stimulant drugs**. That was when I began to understand more about stimulants.

I did have mild diabetes, for which he prescribed local medicine. However, the medicine given for the stomach upset did not work well. The diabetes medication was administered daily, but my blood sugar levels were not monitored at the detention centre due to the lack of medical facilities.

As a detainee, I was subjected to daily interrogations for 20 days. Each session lasted between 3 to 5 hours and was conducted by a single police officer. An interpreter was always present to translate the officer's questions from Japanese to English for me, and my responses from English to Japanese for the officer. This routine became a challenging part of my detention experience.

The investigation was conducted entirely based on the communication found in my emails, WhatsApp messages, and my statements. The investigating officer repeatedly accused me of lying. I responded by saying, "You have all the communication. If I've said anything different, please let me know. Otherwise, you can put me through a lie detector test." The interpreter would indirectly threaten me, implying they had other ways of extracting information from me.

I felt she was threatening me with the possibility of being taken into remand. However, I remained unfazed because I knew I was telling the truth the entire time. ***"The truth will set you free, but first it will piss you off." — Gloria Steinem***

I don't pray because I believe in finding strength and solutions within myself and through my actions. While I respect all religions and the practices associated with them, I prefer to focus on personal responsibility and self-reliance. For me, it's about staying true to my principles and values without relying on external rituals. I just follow three principles of Gautam Buddha.

After the initial days of interrogation, the police officer's focus shifted. He became more interested in learning about India, curious about the country's rapid progress and development. Each day, he would spend over an hour discussing various topics unrelated to the investigation. When he learned about India's progress, I could sense a hint of jealousy on his face. I quickly concluded that his general knowledge was quite poor. He did not know geography. He doesn't read newspapers to stay informed about current events. When I asked him a few questions about the Russia-Ukraine conflict, he was unaware of the situation. It seems he had never travelled outside of Japan and didn't realize that life exists beyond his country. ***This reflected how much a typical Japanese is aware of things outside his world.***

During the interrogation, I was informed that the police had visited the hotel where I was supposed to stay and found a VISA credit card number in my name. This card was provided by Mr. Steven to cover my hotel expenses. Therefore, an ATM card existed in my name. However, they did not visit while Steven was there to pay on my behalf.

The authorities extracted the complete WhatsApp communication and all the emails from my mobile and printed out hard copies. They also translated every communication into Japanese. I could see huge volumes of files with all the agencies investigating the case. Every detail of my trip was very well documented. Given the straightforward nature of the case, it should have been resolved quickly, much like an open-and-shut case. However, the process was prolonged unnecessarily, which added to the stress and complexity of the situation.

In the detention centre, I was allocated a single room. This provided a bit of privacy, but it also added to the isolation and loneliness of the experience.

Detention Centre Routine

7:30 AM – Wake up call daily

8:00 AM – Breakfast

12:00 Noon – Lunch

1:00 PM – 3:00PM – Afternoon Rest Period

4:00 PM – Dinner

8:00 PM – Night Attendance

9:00 PM – Bedtime (Lights Off)

Hot Japanese tea was available throughout the day, which was a small comfort. However, there were very few books in English, making it difficult to pass the time. The weather was quite cold, but the centre was centrally heated, so it was pleasantly warm inside. Unfortunately, the quality and quantity of the food left much to be desired.

They did not permit me to communicate with my family in India, either by phone or message. They claimed to have informed Indian consulate in Osaka, but I had no way to verify this. The Indian consulate came to see me after a week, but he wasn't permitted to speak with me, nor was I allowed to converse with him freely.

This is how an International detainee is treated.

In Japan, communication within the detention system is often kept confidential. All information was relayed through the Japanese officer and interpreter, and only then was my consulate able to inform my family. This added to lack of transparency during my detention. ***From my perspective, this treatment felt inhuman. The secrecy and lack of direct communication added to the emotional strain and isolation, making an already difficult situation even more challenging.***

I passionately assert that international individuals must have unrestricted access to their consulates. This access is crucial for ensuring their rights are protected, providing necessary support, and maintaining communication with their home countries. Denying such access can lead to isolation, increased vulnerability, and a lack of essential legal and emotional assistance.

Despite my requests, the Police Investigator, the interpreter, and the Public Prosecutor did not reveal their names. I was dealing with nameless individuals in human form, which added to my frustration and sense of helplessness.

I was assigned a defense counsel named **Yugo Fukumoto San** to handle my case. He was accompanied by an interpreter to assist with translations. A few days later, Senior Defense Counsel **Tomohire Shibao San** joined forces with Mr. Fukumoto, working together to handle my case. Mr. Shibao was the senior counsel who was asked to lead the case. Two advocates, along with one interpreter worked out the schedule and agreed to meet me every fortnight.

The interpreter also connected with my daughter in India, ensuring my messages reached my family and kept them updated. This dedicated team of defense counsels worked sincerely, keeping me truthfully informed of every action. *From day one until the end, they worked tirelessly and with great dedication.*

The defense team acted as unexpected allies, providing crucial support and guidance throughout the proceedings. Their dedication and efforts were instrumental in ensuring a fair and just process.

The 20-day interrogation was an emotionally draining ordeal, each day intensifying my stress and sense of helplessness. I repeatedly asked the police officer if I was guilty, and each time he responded that he didn't think so. However, he always added that the final decision rested with the Public Prosecutor. The public prosecutor interviewed me twice in the 20 days and to my question, he never said he would convict me. During those 20 days, neither the police nor customs provided me with an explanation of what constitutes a stimulant. The only information I received was from an Indian doctor at the hospital.

On the 20th day, I received a notice of conviction and was informed I would be put on trial.

The public prosecutor has submitted to the court an indictment against me. A criminal trial was hereby called into session. I was charged with the following offences.

1) Violation of the Stimulants Control Act. Article 41, paragraphs 1 and 2 of the said act.
2) Violation of the Customs Act. Article109, paragraphs 3 and 1, Article 69-11, paragraph 1, item (i) of the said Act.
3) Article 60 of the penal code applies to this case as a whole.

Those twenty days were a crucible, strengthening my resolve and preparing me emotionally for the long battle ahead. Each day, filled with uncertainty and stress, taught me resilience and the importance of perseverance, 2 out of 3 principles of Buddha that I have ingrained into my life now.

Initially, the food did not suit me, and I developed a stomach infection. I was taken to a local doctor at the hospital, who advised me to avoid Japanese rice. Although I was given medicine, it did not provide much relief. Over the course of 20 days, I lost about 19-20 kg. During this time, I stopped eating rice and switched to porridge, which gradually provided relief. The Indian doctor at the hospital informed me that the police restrict detailed investigations due to billing concerns. As a result, I had to endure limited treatment. Although I was given local Japanese medicine for my slightly high blood sugar, my sugar levels were never monitored.

In the context of the Japanese judiciary system, it appears that decision-making authority is highly centralized, with only the higher authorities having the freedom to make decisions. This lack of decentralization means that those working at lower levels often operate without the ability to make independent decisions, functioning more like blind followers. Such a system is not conducive to the progress of a developing nation. Many staff members work without the autonomy to make decisions and often restrict access to senior officials. In a growing and developing scenario, it is crucial to decentralize authority to foster a more dynamic and responsive system. The staff managing such a centre should have the authority to make decisions. Although they claim to be concerned about people's health, this is not the case. If they are facing financial issues, they should avoid detaining people for extended periods

I had some basic medicines with me, but they did not allow me to consume them. They prohibited the use of anything I had simply because it was from outside Japan. This reflects an unjustified pride in the belief that only products made in Japan are superior.

Since language is a big problem they must keep sufficient reading material in English. The least they can do is get a daily newspaper to keep detainees occupied. The detainees are not convicts as they are still under investigation. Treating detainees as convicts is against the Geneva Convention. Further Japan must understand that the time to remain isolated and move forward is over. They must learn to live and work as teams. And in such a scenario they must now have few people who can converse in English. In a short period of time I also noticed Japan has been very slow in moving to digital technology. I understood that the older generation is still in command does not want to remove paperwork and move on to digital, which was a bit of shock to me. Japan was always looked upon as a technologically advanced country but reality was different. Few people do use technology but rarely any user is conversant with how it works.

My feedback is not intended to criticize Japan but to offer fair and constructive suggestions from an outsider's perspective.

Chapter 4

Shifted from Police Detention Centre to Judicial Detention Centre

On the completion of 20 days of Police investigation, the Public Prosecutor issued an order to move me to the Judicial Detention Centre. The Judicial Detention Centre was much better compared to the Police Detention Centre. The rooms were clean and self-sufficient. The centre had a full-fledged medical centre with good facilities. The daily routine was also different and much better compared to police detention centre.

The food quality and quantity were much better than at the police detention center. I had the privilege of receiving 16 English books every two weeks, which was an excellent facility. This allowed me to expand my knowledge across various subjects. I learned many things, particularly about Japanese systems, traditions, and culture

Three times a week, there was a half-hour external exercise session, which occasionally reduced to twice a week due to weather conditions like rain. However, I managed to stay active by exercising in my room. We were also allowed to shave and bathe three times a week. The showers were excellent, providing good hot and cold water under pressure. Additionally, the facility had a fully equipped general and dental hospital with all major equipment. The dentist would visit only on Thursdays. The major issue was the language barrier. There was one officer who spoke English, and when I asked for his name, he told me to call him "Englishman." He mentioned that I could request the detention manager to send a message on my behalf. This was a significant relief, as it allowed me to communicate more effectively. Despite being a busy senior executive, he was very helpful throughout my stay. Additionally, each detainee had their own separate room. The common facility was a shower bathroom. Everyone is allowed to take a bath three times a week. Three times a week your clothes were washed by the detention centre. We had the privilege of afternoon nap from 1 PM to 3 PM on our bed, as bedding was kept in the room only.

I anticipated that the trial would conclude quickly. However, this was not to be the case. I was quite surprised and a bit disheartened when my defense counsel informed me that the start of the trial would be delayed. I had hoped for a swift resolution, whether it meant being relieved or convicted. The unexpected delay added to the uncertainty and stress of the situation.

But my senior counsel Shibao San explained the situation very frankly. He said firstly there will be delay because the Public Prosecutor who was handling the case and had asked for my conviction has been transferred. A new Public prosecutor had taken over and he needed to go through all the details which would take about 3-4 months. He informed me that my trial would take place under Sai-ban in the System. The reader needs to understand the Sai-ban system. I shall explain it below.

Saiban-in System

The Saiban-in system that commenced on May 21, 2009, is a system in which the Saiban-in who have been selected from the general public participate in criminal trials for serious cases. The saiban-in, with professional judges, determines whether the defendant is guilty or not and sentences where guilty.

With this system, the justice system will be more familiar to the people.

The Ministry of Justice has been implementing public relations activities on the system so that the people will be able to deepen their understanding.

Appointment Procedure

Around November
Persons who have been selected by lot as next year's candidates for saiban-in will be notified of their selection.
✤At this stage the candidates do not need to appear in the court.

About six weeks before the trial
The candidates who have been further selected by lot for each trial will be notified of the date for appearance by the service of the writ of summons.

The day of the appointment procedure
Six saiban-in will be appointed through the appointment procedure at the court.

Duty of saiban-in

Trial
Saiban-in hear the witness testimony and examine the evidence.

Deliberations
Saiban-in and professional judges deliberate and determine together whether the defendant is guilty or not and the sentence where guilty.

Judgment
The presiding judge renders the judgment.

A courtroom for Saiban-in trials

During my trial, the Jury consisted of three Judges from the Fukuoka District Court and six members from the Public.

Hence it was not known when the trial will start. My counsel kept explaining me every fortnight the methodology being planned to defend me. Looking at the data available it needed a lot of time for the counsel to understand the background. We would have a fortnightly meeting to argue discussing various option and then collectively decide on every step.

I would also like to highlight here the process Japan District laid down and followed it. I was given the schedule in writing that there would be a session presided by the main Judge to read the charge against me. I will be asked to be present. Followed by that will be a pre-trial session in which the evidence to be argued upon will be listed by both the Public Prosecutor and the Defense Counsel. Once the list of evidence is agreed there will be no new evidence allowed to be added. Thereafter the trial date will be scheduled and the Judgement date will be announced.

Based on the feedback from my defense counsel I could estimate that my trial will start no earlier than November 2023. I prepared myself for this long stay. I started to enjoy my food. I had issues with my upper denture, which started causing me discomfort. The dentist promptly attended to my case and initially provided mild medication. When the problem persisted, he prescribed mild antibiotics, which ultimately gave me complete relief.

One evening after dinner, I experienced a severe bout of vomiting. The next day, the doctor examined me, administered a bottle of saline, and performed an ultrasound to diagnose the issue. He also began monitoring my sugar levels. I mentioned experiencing shivering at night, which I suspected was due to low blood sugar. Consequently, he discontinued my diabetic medication.

He monitored my sugar levels weekly, and for nearly six months, my sugar remained under control without any medication. I was thrilled, and even at the time of writing this book, my sugar levels were still stable without any medicine. The medical facility at this detention center was excellent.

As my detention continued, the library's supply of English books was insufficient. So, I decided to start reading an English newspaper. I asked my defense counsel to arrange a daily subscription for me. He managed to set it up, but when the first copy arrived, it was handed to me only after two days. When I inquired about the delay, I was told, "The newspaper needs to be audited before it can be given to the detainee."

I was shocked to learn that even a local Japanese newspaper was subject to such scrutiny, as the authorities did not trust the publisher. They suspected that the newspaper might publish news harmful to the country. Additionally, I was surprised by the price of the newspaper, which was **150 YEN**. I immediately asked my defense counsel to cancel my subscription. This experience helped me understand why people might avoid reading newspapers to stay updated with political news.

It's hard to see how a country can progress when it harbours such deep suspicions about its own establishments. By keeping newspaper prices high, it seems they aim to discourage people from staying informed about world politics. I occasionally bought

juice from the internal store, and the price I paid for 200ml was what I would pay for a litre back home. This local pride in domestic products leads to higher costs, as they avoid importing and instead force people to pay more for local goods.

When I was informed about the reason for the trial delay, I asked my defense counsel if the new prosecutor did not wish to meet me. It would be easier for him to understand the case if he met me and asked questions, as he might get lost just by reading the communication. However, he never called me. Upon analyzing, I concluded that this might work in my favor, so I did not insist on meeting the new public prosecutor.

On the 19 September 2023, I received the notification mentioning the trial will start on 7 November 2023. There were two meetings in the court before the start of the final trial. The first was to confirm the charge as stated by the public prosecutor and the second was the pre-trial to admit the evidences, from the prosecution and defence side on which the trial will be based. The presiding judge made it very clear that no other evidence would be admitted beyond those listed in the pre-trial session. I was allowed to be present in both meetings and was just an observer. It was confirmed the trial will last until 10 November 2023 and Judgement will be given on 15 November 2023.

The weeks leading up to the final trial were incredibly hectic. My defense team met with me weekly, and we rigorously discussed our strategy. These meetings were very productive, fostering healthy discussions between myself and the legal team. By the end of each session, we had a clear understanding of who was right, who was wrong, and which strategy we would follow.

During these few weeks, two significant things happened. Firstly, time seemed to pass very quickly. Secondly, I became well-prepared to face the trial without fear, nervousness, or hesitation. It felt like a normal routine, and I remained calm by adhering to Gautam Buddha's three principles: Truth, Benevolence, and Tolerance. –

"Endurance is one of the most difficult disciplines, but it is to the one who endures that the final victory comes." – Gautam Buddha

Chapter 5

Judicial Detention

After 20 days of interrogation at the police detention centre, I got a notice of conviction from the district court at the request of the public prosecutor. I was moved into judicial detention immediately.

It's truly striking to consider Japan's conviction rate. This is something that simply cannot be overlooked. In Japan, the conviction rate is 99.8 to 99.9%. Public Prosecutor only convicts when he is sure to win the case. This information was collected from one of the books I read at the centre. Having read such a draconian statement I kept calm and made up my mind that I would fight very boldly without any apologies or request for pardon.

My defense counsel was very frank in briefing me in detail, truthfully sharing his experience. I was informed that the public prosecutor who had initially convicted me for trial has been transferred. A new public prosecutor had now taken over the case. Due to this routine shift, which occurs every three years, it took more time before a hearing could start.

All my belongings were taken into custody, including my mobile phone, for which I provided the unlocking code. The authorities copied all my communications from WhatsApp, emails, and other sources. They then translated every word into Japanese and printed hard copies.

I was shocked to see the volume of data Japanese authorities printed out. Copies were made for different departments to go through and prepare for trial. One set of printouts was also with my defence counsel. I could visualise going through it, verifying with me clarifications, and understanding the whole communication was no easy task with language being a barrier.

My defence counsel had numerous clarifications and would meet with me every fortnight and we would sit for hours discussing the approach to trial.. I can only imagine the challenges faced by the investigation authorities.

As I mentioned, they took away all my belongings, including some medicines I had carried. The only thing they allowed me to keep was my undergarments. I had undergone retinal detachment surgery and was using Ayurvedic medicine to help restore my vision to near normal. Even that was not allowed. The Japanese doctor provided some local medicine, but it proved to be useless. ***Yes, I must say that the product made in India was far superior to the Japanese one. Ayurveda is truly one of India's greatest gifts to the world.***

I would like to highlight a few things that, from my perspective, were so absurd they could have been part of

a comedy sketch! They would not allow you to use a track pant which has a thread so that detainee must not commit suicide. I normally use dental floss to clean my teeth after the last meal. They would not allow me to have that. I found a piece of thread four inches long and would use that. Every fortnight they would do room inspection. They caught hold of that thread and took it away saying you can commit suicide. But they didn't realize that the vest they provided could easily be used for a dramatic exit. I used to laugh and tell them ***"Duds please use common sense logic". In return I would get a smile and a polite thank you***

The long journey had just begun. I held tightly to the three principles of Gautam Buddha: Truth, Benevolence, and Tolerance. Yet, the most challenging part was figuring out how to endure the endless hours of isolation and loneliness. No one to talk to. No one to discuss anything. Cut off from the outside world. I decided to keep reading as much as I could. Since I was allowed 16 books every fortnight in English my reading problem was resolved. I saw I could spend my time very comfortably reading on varied subjects. I read many autobiographies of leading leaders, Hollywood actors, war, terror, suspense, murders, mafia, movies, culture, evolution, history, science, and mathematics. Reading along with my regular outdoor and indoor exercise activities kept me going. Some time was spent deciding on the past fortnight discussion with my counsellor and any new ideas arising in my mind which could help in my trial.

Over time, the number of English books in the detention center library was exhausted. So, I asked my defence counsel to start a newspaper subscription for me. He got me a copy of an English newspaper published in Japan and arranged for a subscription. I received the newspaper two days after it was delivered to the detention centre. *I inquired about the delay and I was told it had to be audited 100% so that no unwanted news is published. I also noticed that the cost of Newspaper was 150 Yen. It surprised me that the authorities did not trust even their publications that they needed 2 days to audit the newspaper. The purpose of the Newspaper is dissolved. Secondly, I got my answer as to why a typical Japanese young man is unaware of political information as he cannot afford to read a newspaper costing 150 Yen daily. In my country the leading newspaper daily costs RS6 which translates into 10 Japanese Yen!* I immediately had to stop the newspaper subscription.

As days went by, I found myself analysing my case, contemplating the next steps if I were convicted and what to do if I were acquitted. When I discussed this with my defence counsel, he provided me with a realistic picture of the situation. **I'm sharing this in lawyer's words because it's crucial for everyone to understand.** My defence lawyer stated

A) In case of acquittal

(1) Criminal trial-The public prosecutor could appeal to the higher court until November 29 2023. If the prosecutor appealed, the case would be tried in the Higher court. If

the prosecutor decided not to appeal, the not guilty verdict becomes final after November 29 2023

For the trial in the higher court, please refer to (3) below.

(2) Physical Detention

Your detention will expire upon a verdict of acquittal. However. you cannot legally stay in Japan and will be immediately detained at the Immigration Bureau.

An Immigration Bureau official will be present at the hearing on the date of the verdict, and you will be taken directly to the Immigration Bureau after the verdict is handed down.

After being detained at the immigration office. coordination of deportation proceedings will proceed. You will be returned to India. with the exceptions noted below. The number of days for adjustment depends on the case. In this case, it may take a few days due to

(1) [Exception] – If the prosecutor appeals the judgment of acquittal. you may be detained again. If you are detained again, you will be transferred from the immigration office to the detention centre (where you are now). If your acquittal is upheld after your trial in a higher court. Your detention will expire and you will again be detained at the Immigration Office.

There is some debate among legal experts about remand after acquittal. We would like to express our opinion to the court so that you will not be detained again (so that you can return to India), but we need your own sincere cooperation. Please read this letter to the end and cooperate if you have no problem.

2. In case of conviction

(1) Criminal Trial

You have until November 29 2023 to appeal to the Higher court. If you appeal, the trial will be held in the Higher court. If you do not appeal, your conviction will become final and your sentence will be carried out as of November 29 2023. Of course, you will appeal. and we (The lawyers in this case) will file the petition for appeal.

However. we will discuss with you when to file the appeal. It is possible to appeal immediately. but there is the following problem. Under the law. I and Attorney Fukumoto have the authority to represent you until the "filing" of an appeal. After the petition for appeal is filed, a new counsel is appointed by the higher court. In other words, we cease to be defence counsel the moment we file an appeal.

We have been able to meet with you under the authority of counsel, confidentially have access to you without the presence of detention center officer. and have been able to cover the cost of an interpreter. After the filing of the appeal, this will no longer be possible and our correspondence, including our interactions with your family will cease. After filing an appeal. you will be assigned another counsel in the Higher court but since you may still wish to communicate with us after the judgment, we will consider filing an appeal with your approval.

(2) Physical Detention

After the appeal. your current detention status will continue.

(3) Trial by High Court

(I) Trial System In the event of a conviction, a new attorney will be appointed to represent you in the Higher court. This is because they have the advantage of examining the case from a new perspective. As a general rule, there will be one person, but in some cases, a second person may be appointed for this case. The date on which the new counsel will meet with you will be decided by that new counsel. and we do not know. Generally, we will meet with you after reviewing the case record, so there may be days when you will not be able to see your counsel for a while. In addition. each attorney will make his or her own decisions about how to handle your interactions with your family. It is not a matter of course to be addressed. In a high court trial, the court examines the validity of the judgement of the District Court. It does not start the trial all over again. nor does it continue the trial. It is somewhat inaccurate, but it is similar to a Video Assistant Referee (VAR) in sports.

The person filing the appeal argues in writing that the decision of the court of first instance was wrong. This document is called the statement of the reason for appeal "Kouso Syuisho" The "Kouso Syuisho" must be filed by a certain deadline.

If the prosecutor appeals against a judgment of acquittal. the prosecutor submits the Kouso Syuisho. If the defendant appeals against a judgment of conviction, the newly appointed defence counsel prepares and submits the form.

The opposing party may then file a response to the statement of reasons for appeal (Kouso Syuisho). This can be submitted in the form of an answer and counterclaims "Toubensho" or orally at the trial date. If the prosecutor appeals from the judgment of acquittal, the defence counsel will argue the case. The defence usually submits a "Toubensho"

At a trial in a higher court, both sides arguments are reviewed on the first date, and a date for sentencing is often assigned. Of course. the specifics will vary from case to case. You will receive an explanation from the defence counsel at that time.

(2) Prosecutor's appeal against acquittal and deportation

If you are not detained again and are deported (i.e.. you return to India), your defence counsel will be appointed to represent you in Japan and a trial in a higher court will be conducted. There is no obligation for the defendant to appear for the High Court trial. So there is no need to come to Japan unless there is a special reason.

However, the trial will take place, and your attorney at that time will need to communicate with you and figure out how to respond. In some cases. The higher court may contact you.

We are aware that you came to Japan without knowing that drugs were concealed in the suitcase. However, it is a fact that you came to Japan of your own volition, and you are in a position to respect the Japanese judicial system.

Therefore, you must respond in good faith to any inquiries from your counsel or the court. You should not ignore inquiries from defence counsel or the court, judging for yourself that there is no point in going to trial.

If you sincerely promise to respond in good faith when you are contacted by defence counsel or the court, you will be asked to sign and finger-stamp a document pledging to do so.

This is the nature of the cooperation we are asking for from you. If it is going to be a token pledge. we will decline it. We ask for your heartfelt pledge. We will prepare a new written document for you, so please think carefully about it.

* What it means to respond in good faith It means that you should respond to our documents. e-mails. and voice communications.

Chapter 6

The Trial Begins

Nine long months passed in isolated detention, each day blending into the next. Finally, the day arrived for the trial to begin. The anticipation, the anxiety, and the hope all converged in this moment.

The trial dates fixed were from 7th November 2023 to 10th November 2023. The judgement date was 15 November 2023.

7th November 2023

I dressed in my finest, ready to face whatever fate had in store for me. I was escorted to the court under great secrecy. At 10 AM, the Judge and the jury entered the courtroom, and the hearing started. ***The discipline of the Japanese in adhering to timelines is truly remarkable. Punctuality is deeply ingrained in Japanese culture and is considered a sign of respect and reliability.***

The public prosecutor read the charge against me. ***In Japan, public prosecutors hold significant authority, overseeing investigations, deciding on prosecutions, and ensuring the integrity of the judicial process.***

My defence counsel began by introducing me. I had prepared to introduce myself, but the system was different from what I expected. Instead, my defense counsel asked me questions, and I had to respond with yes or no answers. It was a lengthy process. I was asked which language I preferred for the trial, and I chose English. An experienced interpreter was present, translating every question from my defence counsel into English and then translating my responses back in Japanese

The introduction session lasted until lunchtime and was very well-structured. A thorough introduction was provided, with only a few questions from the jury, all of which were answered effectively. I don't think I could have introduced myself any better. I was quite surprised that the public prosecutor did not ask any questions.

My case was solely based on the communication between Rev. Paul Dalibor and me. It was challenging to draw conclusions just from the translated English communication into Japanese. I made a mental note of this and kept it in mind for my defence as the trial progressed.

We had a two-hour lunch break at noon, but the meal was disappointing. The court reconvened at 2 PM, and the trial continued. The post-lunch session was dedicated to the prosecutor's cross-examination and presenting his evidence.

I braced myself for the toughest questions, knowing the gravity of the charges against me. However, as the trial progressed, I found myself growing increasingly relaxed. I could sense the judge's discomfort with the prosecutor's line of questioning, which gave me a sense of reassurance. The prosecutor merely displayed copies of my WhatsApp messages instead of asking firm questions. I noticed the jury seemed a bit confused. Additionally, I observed the judge rejecting the prosecutor's statements three times, even though they weren't translated into English.

This session was supposed to last for two hours, but the judge halted the trial at 3 PM, instructing the prosecutor to come better prepared the next day to resume the cross-examination. The interruption had a significant impact on my state of mind. Initially, I felt a mix of relief and anxiety. Relief, because the judge's decision to halt the trial suggested that the prosecutor's preparation was inadequate. *Anxiety, because it meant another day of uncertainty and stress. However, knowing that the judge was not satisfied with the prosecutor's approach gave me a sense of hope and reassurance. The uncertainty and the constant shifts between hope and anxiety can be incredibly draining. Talking to my lawyer helped me stay grounded.*

Day 1 of the trial concluded successfully, and I felt satisfied. After the trial, my defence counsel would visit the detention centre and spend two hours discussing the agenda for the next day. He would seek my opinion and share his thoughts on the day's proceedings. He would also alert me to any specific questions raised by the prosecutor. My counsel was pleased with my clear and confident responses, noting that I wasn't nervous about anything

8th November 2023

At 10 AM, the trial resumed, giving the prosecutor time until lunch to cross-examine me. However, much to my frustration, he once again merely displayed copies of my WhatsApp messages without posing any serious questions. This repetitive approach left me feeling both relieved and exasperated. It was evident to me that the prosecutor was confused and unsure about how to secure a conviction.

I discovered that the conviction rate in Japan for serious criminal cases is between 99.8% and 99.9%. Typically, prosecutors only pursue cases when they are confident of securing a conviction. This might explain why the prosecutor seemed confused. As a result, this session felt calm for me, and I was quite relaxed by lunchtime. I just wished we had a better lunch.

After lunch, the session was dedicated to my defence counsel's cross-examination and presentation of evidence. His explanations were precise and scientific, making a compelling case in my favour. He asked me to demonstrate how I checked the bag at Doha before agreeing to carry it. I confidently performed the demonstration, showcasing my thoroughness and attention to detail. I was later told it was an impressive and convincing demonstration.

There were also a few questions from the jury, which I answered. This session was both hectic and interesting.

By the end of the day's trial, all cross-examinations were completed. The next day was reserved for the closing statements from both the public prosecutor and the defence counsel.

As this phase ended, I felt relieved and hopeful. The cross-examinations were done, and I was looking forward to the closing statements, knowing they were crucial. I felt optimistic because of my defence counsel's strong performance and the positive feedback on my demonstration.

9th **November 2023**

The morning session was allocated to the public prosecutor. He meticulously justified his decision to proceed with the trial, presenting each piece of evidence and explaining why he believed it was valid. He even introduced additional evidence that had not been listed in the trial. The judge promptly interrupted him, refusing to accept any explanations. I could see the prosecutor's face flush with humiliation. The judge quickly interrupted and refused to accept the prosecutor's explanations. ***Seeing the prosecutor's face flush with humiliation was a powerful moment. This shift in dynamics visibly weakened the prosecutor's stance and boosted my confidence.*** In the end, the prosecutor passionately insisted that I should face 10 years of hard labour and a fine of four million Japanese Yen. **It was incredibly challenging to hear such a statement!**

Any normal person would have felt nervous hearing the prosecutor's recommendation. However, I remained composed and dismissed his feedback, given his handling of the trial. We then proceeded to lunch. My inner conscience reassured me not to worry. I had immense trust in the capabilities of my defence counsel, having spent many days together discussing our trial strategy & observing his presentation.

After lunch, it was time for the defence counsel to deliver his closing statement. He presented methodical explanations, backing each piece of evidence with concrete reasoning. He thoroughly considered my background, work experience, and age in his arguments. **The atmosphere in the courtroom was tense yet attentive**. As the defence counsel methodically presented his closing statement, you could sense the anticipation and focus from everyone present. Each point he made seemed to resonate, creating a palpable sense of hope and determination within me. The defence counsel concluded with a strong recommendation for my acquittal

The next day, it was my turn to give my statement. I asked my defence counsel if I would be speaking on my own or if it would be like the introduction session. He informed me that I would have to speak on my own.

10th November

I began by stating that I would first list the charges filed against me. If the Judge and Jury agreed, I would then proceed with my statement. The Judge and Jury seemed attentive and respectful of my approach. They listened carefully as i outlined the charges as stated below

1) I have been charged for bringing in a stimulant which is a banned item, for monetary gain.
2) The trip to Japan was offered subject to my carrying the gift bag.

Upon their acceptance, I proceeded with a brief explanation as follows; – "The whole case is based on communication that has been downloaded and translated into Japanese. Nowhere, I repeat, nowhere is it mentioned that I would only be given this trip if I carried the gift suitcase. Hence, the charge that this trip was to carry the bag containing stimulants for monetary benefit is false. In my communication, I had mentioned to Rev Paul Dalibor that I would inspect the bag at Doha airport and if I find anything hidden I shall not carry it. I checked the bag by removing all the clothes. I checked every piece of cloth for anything hidden inside the pockets or in the seams. I then checked the bag from all sides, outside and inside to see if any modification was done or if it was heavier than a normal bag. I did not find anything, then I tapped the bag from all sides to see if I could hear any unexpected sound of any hidden material. I did not find anything. Further, since this bag was carried by Mr Micheal from Ohio on his way to Israel it must have undergone an X-ray scan, so I decided to carry the bag.

At the Fukuoka customs even the expert inspectors who do scanning day in and day out could not find out anything just via scan. They were able to see just a black screen. I on my own gave my consent in writing to cut the bag and see what is it. If I had even slight inclination I would not have given my consent on my own.

Additionally, I suggested to customs that they send someone to the hotel, as there was a person named Mr. Stephen who was supposed to pay for my stay and collect the bag. This would have allowed them to determine the exact destination of the stimulant. However, they ignored my suggestion for reasons known only to them.

Therefore, based on the above, I acknowledge that some banned material was brought along with me, but it was unintentional. If the Judge and Jury find me guilty, I will accept the punishment. I also want to take this opportunity to thank the Judges and the Jury."

The trial concluded at lunchtime, and I was taken back to the detention centre. I had my lunch there, which was surprisingly much better than the meal at the trial court. While having lunch, I was reflecting on the closing remarks of both the Public Prosecutor and the defence counsel. I was closely observing the facial expressions of the jury. *As I munched on my lunch, I found myself laughing at the closing remarks of the public prosecutor who demanded 10 years imprisonment and fine of 4 million Japanese Yen (equivalent to 24 Lakhs Indian Rupees), Has he lost his mind, I wondered ? Doesn't he realize that the honourable judge warned him multiple times to come prepared for his questions?*

I was also observing the facial expressions of the jury and concluded that they would declare me innocent. The judge's remarks, warning the prosecutor, clearly indicated his disagreement with the prosecutor's statements. Naturally, the closing arguments from my defence counsel were entirely in my favour.

After finishing my lunch, I realized I had to wait a full five days before the judgment would be delivered. Following lunch, I would take a two-hour afternoon nap, as permitted. I lay down and was about to drift into a nice nap when an officer came and informed me that I had been called for an interview. I followed him to the interview room, where an officer was speaking in Japanese. He had a mobile interpreter who would translate his questions into English. I would give my answer and she would translate it into Japanese and then the officer would note it down.

The first question I was asked was:

Officer: "Your trial is over and you have been given 10 years of imprisonment and 4 million YEN as a fine? How do you feel?"

Nanda: "May I know who is taking this interview"

Interpreter: "I am from the director's office"

Nanda: "May I have the name of the director so that I can meet him"

Interpreter: "No that is not allowed"

Nanda: *"Mam you and your director are stupid humans who do not even understand Japanese forget about English. The trial is over and the judgement is scheduled to be given on 15 November 2024 at 2.30 PM. I shall appreciate if you and your director is present there to hear the judgement so that after that I can slap both of you and make a black sheep in front of different people including the press. Show to the public how the director's office tries to make detainees nervous. So I hope now you know how am I feeling after the trial. I am very clear that based on the trial I will be declared innocent which may be a shock for your prosecutor. Yes, he can file an appeal in the High Court."*

I didn't understand the purpose of this interview, but I had a strong sense that it was orchestrated by the prosecutor to gauge my reaction. Despite this, the teachings of Gautam Buddha, which I deeply follow, kept me calm and composed. However, I couldn't shake off a feeling of racism.

However, I remained in high spirits for several reasons. The most thrilling aspect was that my case could result in a unique decision in the history of the Japanese judicial system, where the conviction rate is between 99.8% and 99.9%. I was anticipating that the judgment would be delivered by voting immediately after the trial.

However, my defence counsel corrected me, explaining that the decision would be thoroughly discussed with the judges, ensuring no partiality. If I have any doubts or concerns, I can appeal to the High Court within 14 days. Similarly, if the Public Prosecutor believes the judgment is incorrect, he can also appeal to the High Court. Therefore, please be aware that the judgment on November 15, 2024, is not final but is a clear decision of the trial court.

With the trial behind me, a wave of relief washed over. Now, all that remained was to await the verdict that would shape the course of my future.

Chapter 7

Judgement

The five days following the trial flew by quickly. During this time, I had only one interaction with my defence counsel, who provided me with a few instructions. He advised me to pack my belongings without knowing the judgment and to keep the detention centre items separate in the room. If I were acquitted, I wouldn't be allowed to return to my room. With the judgment scheduled for 2:30 PM, I had plenty of time to follow his advice meticulously.

I had my final lunch at the detention centre, and it was a good meal. After brushing my teeth, as I always do after eating, I was moved to the court at 1:30 PM. All eyes were on me, like dragon eyes, as everyone seemed convinced that I would receive a harsh punishment. ***You can imagine the weight of the world looking at you as guilty, with no one to talk to because of language barriers. It takes immense strength to endure such a situation. The teachings of Gautam Buddha gave me the strength to confront the harsh realities of a world far from my hometown, in a country thousands of miles away. He became a beacon of light, guiding my path and strengthening my belief in his teachings.***

I had initially expected that the jury would deliver a verbal judgment with a vote immediately after the trial. However, I was informed that the decision would be made jointly by the judges and the jury in a closed room, with the judgment to be declared on November 15, 2023, at 2:30 PM.

For the next five days, a single thought kept troubling me: since the decision was being made behind closed doors, there was a lingering fear that it might not be fair. This uncertainty weighed heavily on my mind. Despite my concerns, I realized there was nothing more I could do to influence the outcome. I had to place my trust in the process and prepare myself to accept whatever the final judgment would be.

My family, especially my daughter, who has been following the case with unwavering dedication, was anxiously awaiting the judgment. Her hope and concern have been a constant source of strength for me during this difficult time.

Sharp at 2.30 PM the Judges along with the members of Jury entered the court and the Judge started to read the judgement. I was ultra-attentive as I had to follow the translation since the Judgement was being read in Japanese.

The judge's first statement was, **"The defendant is not guilty."** I glanced at my defence counsel and saw a glimmer of success in his expression, a ray of light that signalled our victory.

In that moment, a wave of relief and joy washed over me. Hearing the words "The defendant is not guilty" felt surreal. I glanced at my defence counsel and saw the glimmer of success in his expression, which only amplified my emotions. It was as if a heavy burden had been lifted off my shoulders, and I could finally breathe freely again. The support and hope from my family, especially my daughter, flashed through my mind, making the victory even more meaningful.

Given Japan's 99.9% conviction rate, this must have been a significant achievement for the defence counsel. I paid little attention to the rest of the judgment, instead focusing intently on the public prosecutor's facial expression. It was as if the sky had fallen for him. With such a high conviction rate, it's rare for a public prosecutor to lose a case, especially one as serious as mine. The judgment was a shock to him. His closing statement recommended a fine of four million YEN and ten years of rigorous imprisonment. I could sense he was instructing his assistant to prepare for an appeal in the higher court and I was proven right later.

The complete judgment process lasted approximately 90 to 110 minutes, and then the trial concluded.

Immediately, I was surrounded by immigration authorities, a representative from the Indian Consulate in Osaka, and my defence counsel. The Indian consular and my defense counsel informed me that they would accompany me to the immigration centre. I was taken back to the detention centre, and as my defence counsel had informed me, I was not allowed to return to my detention room. My belongings were brought down, and I was handed all my confiscated items material. It took us an hour to get the things packed and we drove down to the immigration detention centre.

At the immigration center, I received new instructions. I was surprised that even there, very few people spoke broken English, but I had grown accustomed to it as a way of life. Later in the evening, the Indian consular and my defence counsel came to meet me. They gathered all the necessary information to prepare my travel documents since my passport had expired.

I must alert fellow Indian citizens that the services of our consular are quite unsatisfactory. During my nine months of detention, the consular met me only four times. One must be prepared to handle things independently in a foreign land. I informed the court about the expiration of my passport, visa, and return ticket. The court assured me that these issues would be addressed at the time of deportation. However, the immigration authorities regretted to inform me that they currently lacked the funds for my return ticket, and it would take time for approval. Until then, I would have to remain in detention.

It is important to note such decisions made by the authorities in the end. One should not rely on verbal assurances, as they may not be honoured. Despite my acquittal, I requested permission to go around the city and do some shopping for my family, but my request was denied. This experience revealed the true nature of the investigation. Even after being acquitted, I was treated differently.

My defence counsel informed my daughter about the judgment and the next steps. I was allowed to make the first phone call to my family after nearly 9 months. Hearing their voices after such a long and difficult time brought a wave of relief and joy. My daughter informed me that she has sent the money to the defence counsel, who would hand it over to immigration to purchase my return ticket. ***Knowing that I'll soon be reunited with my loved ones filled me with hope and gratitude.***

Chapter 8

Post Judgement

On November 15, 2023, at 4:30 PM, I was taken back to the detention centre and placed in the custody of immigration. I wasn't allowed to visit my room or say goodbye to the people I had spent over nine months with. All my confiscated belongings were returned to me, and I was then taken to the immigration detention centre. The language barrier continued at the immigration detention centre. I was given a room and began the final part of my stay. As planned, my defence counsel and an Indian Consulate official visited me. I provided the necessary information to get temporary travel documents. Although the consular had promised to renew my passport two months ago, he refused to acknowledge my emails at the last moment. He promised to send the temporary travel documents within three days but failed to do so. My daughter had to contact authorities in New Delhi to urge our consulate official in Osaka to expedite the documents.

We met with the immigration officer to discuss getting my return ticket quickly. The officer regretted that they didn't have funds at the moment and that approval would take time. My defence counsel advised that I could legally return to India even if the Public Prosecutor appealed to the High Court. If the appeal was accepted, I might be detained again until the case was resolved, which could take a long time. So, my daughter sent the money for the return ticket immediately. It's clear that even the Japanese authorities didn't honour their commitments.

Despite everything, I had to stay for another week. As expected, the Public Prosecutor immediately filed an appeal in the High Court. After reviewing the case, the High Court rejected the appeal and sent it back to the trial court for review in March 2024. On May 15, 2024, the trial court dismissed the Public Prosecutor's appeal. Given the dismissals, the prosecutor did not pursue further appeal to the Supreme Court. The case was officially closed on May 31, 2024. My defence counsel has filed an application for compensation, and we are now awaiting the decision.

I bid farewell to Japan's land, its grace. On the 23rd November 2023, I took to the skies, heading homeward, to be reunited with my family.

On my way back, I reflected on the lessons I learned from this experience. Staying calm and composed, even in the face of adversity, can lead to positive outcomes. The guidance and expertise of my legal counsel was instrumental in my acquittal. The unwavering support from my family, was vital. Their efforts to ensure my return and their emotional support were key to getting through this tough time. This experience provided deep insights into the Japanese judicial system, known for its high conviction rates. It underscored the complexities and challenges within the legal process. Despite the hardships, finding moments of gratitude and compassion, whether towards those who supported me was incredibly healing.